A gift for:

_____

From:

_____

YOU!

God's Brand-New Idea

Made to Be Amazing

MAX LUCADO

Contents

Made for God's Plan

Made to Be Loved by God

Made to Love God

Preface

Dear friend,

"You need to be more like your brother."
"To get ahead, you'll need the skills of your boss."
"If you try harder, you can be anything you want to be."
Sound familiar? People like to change you. God, however, wants you to be you, the best you can be! "Each of us is an original!" (Gal. 5:26 MSG). He placed within you a unique-to-you design. Quarry it and you honor him and enjoy yourself.

I hope these writings will prompt you toward that goal. They come from a variety of my books and cooperate to make one point: You are God's brand-new idea! He has designed you and gifted you in a unique way so that you can fulfill the special purpose he has in mind for you. Use your giftedness to build your life and your work on God's unique will for YOU!

Your friend,
MAX LUCADO

YOU!

God's Brand-New Idea

Made to Be Amazing

Made by God

Then God said, "Let Us make man in Our image."

GENESIS 1:26 NKJV

Made in God's Image

Imagine God's creativity. Of all we don't know about the creation, there is one thing we do know—he did it with a smile. He must've had a blast. Painting the stripes on the zebra, hanging the stars in the sky, putting the gold in the sunset. What creativity! Stretching the neck of the giraffe, putting the flutter in the mockingbird's wings, planting the giggle in the hyena.

What a time he had. Like a whistling carpenter in his workshop, he loved every bit of it. He poured himself into the work. So intent was his creativity that he took a day off at the end of the week just to rest.

And then, as a finale to a brilliant performance, he made man. With his typical creative flair, he began with a useless mound of dirt and ended up with an invaluable species called a human. A human who had the unique honor to bear the stamp, "In his Image."

No Wonder They Call Him the Savior

Created by God's Hand

B y Him all things were created, both in the heavens and on earth, visible and invisible, whether thrones or dominions or rulers or authorities—all things have been created through Him and for Him" (Col. 1:15–16 NASB).

What a phenomenal list!

Heavens and earth.

Visible and invisible.

Thrones, dominions, rulers, and authorities. No thing, place, or person omitted. The scale on the sea urchin. The hair on the elephant hide. . . . The rain that nourishes the desert, the infant's first heartbeat—all can be traced back to the hand of Christ.

Next Door Savior

God placed his hand on the shoulder of humanity and said, "You're something special."

You knit me

together in

my mother's womb.

No Two Alike

K nitted together" is how the psalmist described the process of God making man. Not manufactured or mass-produced, but knitted. Each thread of personality tenderly intertwined. Each string of temperament deliberately selected.

God as creator. Pensive. Excited. Inventive.

An artist, brush on pallet, seeking the perfect shade.

A composer, fingers on keyboard, listening for the exact chord.

A poet, pen poised on paper, awaiting the precise word.

The Creator, the master weaver, threading together the soul.

Each one different. No two alike. None identical.

Six Hours One Friday

Exceptional!

Fabulous!

YOU

Original!

Unique!

Incomparable!

Wonderful!

God Authored Your Life

M y frame was not hidden from you when I was made in the secret place. When I was woven together in the depths of the earth, your eyes saw my unformed body. All the days ordained for me were written in your book before one of them came to be" (Ps. 139:15–16 NIV). . . .

David emphasizes the pronoun "you" as if to say "you, God, and you alone." "The secret place" suggests a hidden and safe place, concealed from intruders and evil. Just as an artist takes a canvas into a locked studio, so God took you into his hidden chamber where you were "woven together." The Master Weaver selected your temperament threads, your character texture, the yarn of your personality—all before you were born.

What motivates you, what exhausts you . . . God authored—and authors—it all.

Cure for the Common Life

He fashions their

hearts individually.

PSALM 33:15 NKJV

YOU God's Brand-New Idea

What a Good Idea!

You are heaven's custom design.

At a moment before moments existed, the sovereign Star Maker resolved, "I will make _____." Your name goes in the blank. Then he continued with, "And I will make him/her _____, _____ and _____ and _____ and _____." Fill those blanks with your characteristics. Insightful. Clever. Detail oriented. Restless. And since you are God's idea, you are a good idea. What God said about Jeremiah, he said about you: "Before I made you in your mother's womb, I chose you. Before you were born, I set you apart for a special work" (Jeremiah 1:5).

Set apart for a special work.

Cure for the Common Life

Heaven's Halley's Comet

Y ou are the only you God made.

In their book *Behavioral Genetics*, Robert Plomin, J. C. DeFries, and G. E. McClaren declare:

> Each of us has the capacity to generate 10^{3000} eggs or sperm with unique sets of genes. If we consider 10^{3000} possible eggs being generated by an individual woman and the same number of sperm being generated by an individual man, the likelihood of anyone else with your set of genes in the past or in the future becomes infinitesimal.

If numbers numb you, let me simplify. God made you and broke the mold. . . . Every single baby is a brand-new idea from the mind of God.

No one can duplicate your life. Scan history for your replica; you won't find it. God "personally formed and made each one" (Isa. 43:7 MSG). No box of "backup yous" sits in God's workshop. You aren't one of many bricks in the mason's pile or one of a dozen bolts in the mechanic's drawer. You are it! And if you aren't you, we don't get you. The world misses out.

You are heaven's Halley's comet; we have one shot at seeing you shine. You offer a gift to society that no one else brings. If you don't bring it, it won't be brought.

Cure for the Common Life

Custom Designed

You are a custom design; you are tailor-made. God prescribed your birth. Regardless of the circumstances that surrounded your arrival, you are not an accident. God planned you before you were born.

The longings of your heart, then, are not incidental; they are critical messages. The desires of your heart are not to be ignored; they are to be consulted. As the wind turns the weather vane, so God uses your passions to turn your life. God is too gracious to ask you to do something you hate.

Just Like Jesus

We are God's workmanship.

EPHESIANS 2:10 NIV

He has filled them
with skill.

EXODUS 35:35 NKJV

Packed for a Purpose

ou were born prepacked. God looked at your entire life, determined your assignment, and gave you the tools to do the job.

Before traveling, you do something similar. You consider the demands of the journey and pack accordingly. Cold weather? Bring a jacket. Business meeting? Carry the laptop. Time with grandchildren? Better take some sneakers and pain medication.

God did the same with you. *Joe will research animals . . . install curiosity. Meagan will lead a private school . . . an extra dose of management. I need Eric to comfort the sick . . . include a healthy share of compassion. Denalyn will marry Max . . . instill a double portion of patience.*

"Each of us is an original" (Gal. 5:26 MSG). God packed you on purpose for a purpose.

Cure for the Common Life

Your life has a plot;
your years have a theme.

Discover Who You Are

God never prefabs or mass-produces people. No slapdash shaping. "I make all things new," he declares (Rev. 21:5 NKJV). He didn't hand you your granddad's life or your aunt's life; he personally and deliberately packed *you*. . . .

You can do something no one else can do in a fashion no one else can do it. Exploring and extracting your uniqueness excites you, honors God, and expands his kingdom. So "make a careful exploration of who you are and the work you have been given, and then sink yourself into that" (Gal. 6:4 MSG).

Discover and deploy your knacks. . . . When you do the most what you do the best, you put a smile on God's face. What could be better than that?

Cure for the Common Life

Made to Be Unique

Each of us is
an Original.

GALATIANS 5:26 MSG

You Are You-Nique

God made you *you-nique*.

Secular thinking, as a whole, doesn't buy this. Secular society sees no author behind the book, no architect behind the house, no purpose behind or beyond life. Society sees no bag and certainly never urges you to unpack one. It simply says, "You can be anything you want to be."

Be a butcher if you want to, a sales rep if you like. Be an ambassador if you really care. You can be anything you want to be. But can you? If God didn't pack within you the meat sense of a butcher, the people skills of a salesperson, or the world vision of an ambassador, can you be one? An unhappy, dissatisfied one perhaps. But a fulfilled one? No. Can an acorn become a rose, a whale fly like a bird, or lead become gold? Absolutely not. You cannot be anything you want to be. But you can be everything God wants you to be.

Cure for the Common Life

You Can Only Be You

Y ou can't be your hero, your parent, or your big brother. You might imitate their golf swing or hair style, but you can't be them. You can only be you. All you have to give is what you've been given to give. Concentrate on who you are and what you have.

God never called you to be anyone other than you. But he does call on you to be the best *you* you can be.

Cure for the Common Life

Don't compare yourself with others.
Each of you must take responsibility
for doing the creative best
you can with your own life.

GALATIANS 6:4–5 MSG

How would you answer this multiple-choice question?

I am

_____*a coincidental collision of particles.*

_____*an accidental evolution of molecules.*

_____*soulless flotsam in the universe.*

_____*"fearfully and wonderfully made."*

Don't dull your life by missing this point: You are more than statistical chance, more than a marriage of heredity and society, more than a confluence of inherited chromosomes and childhood trauma. More than a walking weather vane whipped about by the cold winds of fate.

Thanks to God you have been "sculpted from nothing into something" (Ps. 139:15 MSG).

Envision Rodin carving *The Thinker* out of a rock. The sculptor chisels away a chunk of stone, shapes the curve of a kneecap, sands the forehead. . . . Now envision God doing the same: sculpting the way you are before you even were, engraving you with

an eye for organization.
an ear for fine music.
a heart that beats for justice and fairness.
a mind that understands quantum physics.
the tender fingers of a caregiver. or
the strong legs of a runner.

Cure for the Common Life

I will praise You, for I am
fearfully and wonderfully made.

PSALM 139:14 NKJV

You Were Made for Your Part

ccept God's permission to be whom he made you to be.

Rick Burgess and Bill "Bubba" Bussey host the wildly popular Rick and Bubba Show, a drive-time radio broadcast that originates in Birmingham, Alabama. Animators once made a cartoon out of the two characters and invited Rick and Bubba to provide the voices. Rick was the voice of Rick, and Bubba, the voice of Bubba. Bubba, however, couldn't seem to please his producer. He suggested that Bubba change inflections, volume, and other details. Bubba grew understandably impatient. After all, he was voicing himself. He turned to the producer and objected, "If I am me, how can I mess me up?"

Great point. When it comes to being you, you were made for the part. So speak your lines with confidence.

Cure for the Common Life

When you do the most
what you do the best,
you pop the pride buttons
on the vest of God.

YOU **God's Brand-New Idea**

Your Personal Knack Sack

God gave you, not a knapsack, but a knack sack. These knacks accomplish results. Maybe you have a knack for managing multitudes of restaurant orders or envisioning solutions to personnel issues. Synonymous verbs mark your biography: "repairing," "creating," "overseeing." Perhaps you decipher things— Sanskrit or football defenses. Maybe you organize things—data or butterflies.

Strengths—you employ them often with seemingly little effort. "God has given each of us the ability to do certain things well" (Rom. 12:6 NLT).

What certain things come to you so easily that you genuinely wonder why others can't do them? Doesn't everyone know the Periodic Table of Elements? Nooooo, they don't. But the fact that you do says much about your strength (not to mention your IQ!).

Cure for the Common Life

Doing What You Do Best

Success is not defined by position or pay scale but by this: doing the most what you do the best. Here is some wise counsel for life:

Do what you love to do so well that someone pays you to do it.

Choose satisfaction over salary. Better to be happy with little than miserable with much.

Pursue the virtue of contentment.

When choosing or changing jobs, be careful. Consult your design. Consult your Designer. But never consult your greed.

What fits others might not fit you.

Let your uniqueness define your path of life.

Cure for the Common Life

YOU **God's Brand-New Idea**

You can do something in a manner that no one else can.

Let's Make God Proud

When our gifts illuminate him and help God's children, don't you think he beams! Let's spend a lifetime making him proud.

Use your uniqueness to do so. You exited the womb called. Don't see yourself as a product of your parents' DNA, but rather as a brand-new idea from heaven.

Make a big deal out of God. Become who you are for him! Has he not transferred you from a dull, death-destined life to a rich, heaven-bound adventure? Remember, "You were chosen to tell about the excellent qualities of God" (1 Pet. 2:9 GOD'S WORD). And do so every day of your life.

A common life? Heaven knows no such phrase. With God, every day matters, every person counts.

And that includes you.

You do something no one else does, in a manner no one else does it. And when your uniqueness meets God's purpose, both of you will rejoice . . . forever.

Cure for the Common Life

YOU **God's Brand-New Idea**

Exceptional!

Fabulous!

YOU

Original!

Unique!

Incomparable!

Wonderful!

Made for God's Purpose

YOU **God's Brand-New Idea**

God Gives Gifts

od cherishes you like Stradivarius would his newest violin. He does! Believe it, and extract your strengths with great joy.

Consider yourself a million-dollar investment—in many cases, a multimillion dollar enterprise.

God gives gifts, not miserly, but abundantly.

And not randomly, but carefully: "to each according to each one's unique ability" (Matt. 25:15 NKJV).

Remember, no one else has your talents. No one. God elevates you from commonhood by matching your unique abilities to custom-made assignments.

Cure for the Common Life

God is working
in you to help you want
to do and be able
to do what pleases him.

PHILIPPIANS 2:13 NCV

Defined by God's Design

uring a college break I made extra money by sweeping metal shavings. Several dozen machinists spent ten hours a day shaping steel at their lathes. Need a six-inch square of quarter-inch sheet metal? They could cut it. Need screw holes in the hinge? They could bore them. The workers shaped the steel according to its purpose. God does the same.

God shaped you according to your purpose. How else can you explain yourself? Your ability to diagnose an engine problem by the noise it makes, to bake a cake without a recipe. How do you explain such quirks of skill?

God. He knew young Israel would need a code, so he gave Moses a love for the law. He knew the doctrine of grace would need a fiery advocate, so he set Paul ablaze. And in your case, he knew what your generation would need and gave it. He designed you. And *his design defines your destiny*.

Cure for the Common Life

Live YOUR Life

The Unseen Conductor prompts this orchestra we call living. When gifted teachers aid struggling students and skilled managers disentangle bureaucratic knots, when dog lovers love dogs and number crunchers zero balance the account, when you and I do the most what we do the best for the glory of God, we are "marvelously functioning parts in Christ's body" (Rom. 12:5 MSG).

You play no small part, because there is no small part to be played. "All of you together are Christ's body, and each one of you is a separate and necessary part of it" (1 Cor. 12:27 NLT). "Separate" and "necessary." Unique and essential. No one else has been given your lines. . . . The Author of the human drama entrusted your part to you alone. Live your life, or it won't be lived.

We need you to be you.
You need you to be you.

Cure for the Common Life

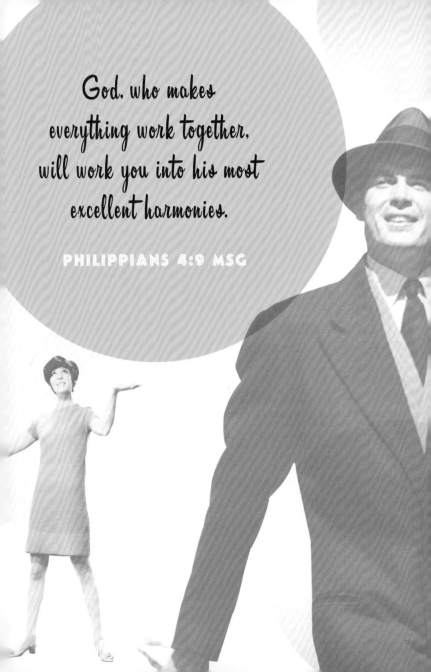

God, who makes everything work together, will work you into his most excellent harmonies.

PHILIPPIANS 4:9 MSG

Exceptional!

Fabulous!

YOU

Original!

Unique!

Incomparable!

Wonderful!

We Need You!

Whether you work at home or in the marketplace, your work matters to God.

And your work matters to society. We need you! Cities need plumbers. Nations need soldiers. Stoplights break. Bones break. We need people to repair the first and set the second. Someone has to raise kids, raise cane, and manage the kids who raise Cain.

Whether you log on or lace up for the day, you imitate God. Jehovah himself worked for the first six days of creation. Jesus said, "My Father never stops working, and so I keep working, too" (John 5:17 NCV).

Your career consumes half of your lifetime. Shouldn't it broadcast God? Don't those forty to sixty hours a week belong to him as well?

The Bible never promotes workaholism or an addiction to employment for pain medication. But God unilaterally calls all the physically able to till the gardens he gives. God honors work. So honor God in your work.

Cure for the Common Life

God Uses the Common

Heaven may have a shrine to honor God's uncommon use of the common.

It's a place you won't want to miss. Stroll through and see Rahab's rope, Paul's bucket, David's sling, and Samson's jawbone. Wrap your hand around the staff that split the sea and smote the rock.

I don't know if these items will be there. But I am sure of one thing—the people who used them will.

The risk takers: Rahab who sheltered the spy. The brethren who smuggled Paul.

The conquerors: David, slinging a stone. Samson, swinging a bone. Moses, lifting a rod.

And the Angels Were Silent

Those who try to keep
their lives will lose them.
But those who give up
their lives will save them.

LUKE 17:33 NCV

It is God himself
who has made us what we are
and given us new lives from
Christ Jesus; and long ages ago he
planned that we should spend these
lives in helping others.

EPHESIANS 2:10 TLB

We are NEVER away from God! He is NEVER away from us—not even for a moment! God doesn't come to us on Sunday mornings and then exit on Sunday afternoons. He remains within us, continually present in our lives.

What incredibly good news for us!

N

ot every teacher should be a principal. Not every carpenter should head a crew. Not every musician should conduct an orchestra. Promotions might promote a person right out of his or her sweet spot. For the love of more, we might lose our purpose.

Just because a king gives you armor, you don't have to wear it. David didn't. When he volunteered to go mano a mano with Goliath, King Saul tried to clothe the shepherd boy with soldier's armor. After all, Goliath stood over nine feet tall. He wore a bronze helmet and a 125-pound coat of mail. He bore bronze leggings and carried a javelin and a spear with a 15-pound head (1 Sam. 17:4–7 NLT). And David? David had a slingshot. This is a VW Bug playing blink with an eighteen-wheeler, a salmon daring the grizzly to

bring it on. When Saul saw David, pimpled, and Goliath, rippled, he did what any Iron Age king would do. "Saul gave David his own armor—a bronze helmet and a coat of mail" (1 Sam. 17:38 NLT).

But David refused it. Look at this wise young man. "David put it on, strapped the sword over it, and took a step or two to see what it was like, for he had never worn such things before. 'I can't go in these,' he protested. 'I'm not used to them.' So he took them off again" (v. 39 NLT).

David rejected the armor, selected the stones, lobotomized the giant, and taught us a powerful lesson: what fits others might not fit you. Indeed what fits *the king* might not fit you. Just because someone hands you armor, you don't have to wear it. Just because someone gives you advice, a job, or a promotion, you don't have to accept it. Let your uniqueness define your path of life. "You, LORD, give perfect peace to those who keep their purpose firm and put their trust in you" (Isa. 26:3 TEV).

Cure for the Common Life

Examine your gifts;
know your strengths.

Have a sane estimate of
your capabilities.

ROMANS 12:3 PHILLIPS

Stay on Target

One of the incredible abilities of Jesus was to stay on target. His life never got off track. . . . He kept his life on course.

As Jesus looked across the horizon of his future, he could see many targets. Many flags were flapping in the wind, each of which he could have pursued. He could have been a political revolutionary. . . . He could have been content to be a teacher and educate minds. . . . But in the end he chose to be a Savior and save souls.

Anyone near Christ for any length of time heard it from Jesus himself. "The Son of Man came to find lost people and save them" (Luke 19:10 NCV). . . . The heart of Christ was relentlessly focused on one task. The day he left the carpentry shop of Nazareth he had one ultimate aim—the cross of Calvary. He was so focused that his final words were, "It is finished" (John 19:30 NCV).

Just Like Jesus

asn't God earned your trust?

Has he ever spoken a word that proved to be false? Given a promise that proved to be a lie? Decades of following God led Joshua to conclude: "Not a word failed of any good thing which the LORD had spoken" (Josh. 21:45 NKJV). Look up reliability in heaven's dictionary and read its one-word definition: God. "If we are faithless he always remains faithful. He cannot deny his own nature" (2 Tim. 2:13 PHILLIPS).

Make a list of his mistakes. Pretty short, eh? Now make a list of the times he has forgiven you for yours. Who on earth has such a record? "The One who called you is

completely dependable. If he said it, he'll do it!"
(1 Thess. 5:24 MSG).

You can depend on him. He is "the same yesterday and today and forever" (Heb. 13:8 ESV). And because he is the Lord, "He will be the stability of your times" (Isa. 33:6 NASB).

Trust him. "But when I am afraid, I put my trust in you" (Ps. 56:3 NLT). Join with Isaiah, who resolved, "I will trust in him and not be afraid" (Isa. 12:2 NLT).

God is directing your steps and delighting in every detail of your life (Ps. 37:23–24 NLT).

Doesn't matter who you are. He is in control.

Come Thirsty

Made to Dream

God can do things that are not possible for people to do.

LUKE 18:27

Dare to Dream

God always rejoices when we dare to dream. In fact, we are much like God when we dream. The Master exults in newness. He delights in stretching the old. He wrote the book on making the impossible possible.

Examples? Check the Book.

Eighty-year-old shepherds don't usually play chicken with Pharaohs . . . but don't tell that to Moses.

Teenage shepherds don't normally have showdowns with giants . . . but don't tell that to David.

Night-shift shepherds don't usually get to hear angels sing and see God in a stable . . . but don't tell that to the Bethlehem bunch.

And for sure don't tell that to God. He's made an eternity out of making the earthbound airborne.

And the Angels Were Silent

You Can Make a Difference

Dare you dream that you can make a difference?

God's answer would be, "Just do something and see what happens."

Begin. Just begin! John F. Kennedy reportedly ordered that an oak tree be planted on the White House lawn. The gardener objected, saying the tree wouldn't mature for a decade. "Then by all means," urged the president, "plant it today." Don't let the size of the task keep you from sowing a seed.

Against a towering giant, a brook pebble seems futile. But God used it to topple Goliath. Compared to the tithes of the wealthy, a widow's coins seem puny. But Jesus used them to inspire us.

Moses had a staff.
David had a sling.
Samson had a jawbone.
Rahab had a string.
Mary had some ointment.
Aaron had a rod.
Dorcas had a needle.
All were used by God.

What do you have?
God inhabits the tiny seed, empowers the tiny deed.
Small deeds can change the world.

Cure for the Common Life

Heed that inner music.
No one else hears it
the way you do.

Whenever you do something you enjoy and believe you do well, you're using some or all of the elements of your giftedness. Record experiences and accomplishments you have enjoyed and note recurring themes.

Unique to You

Da Vinci painted one *Mona Lisa*. Beethoven composed one Fifth Symphony. And God made one version of you. He custom designed you for a one-of-a-kind assignment. Mine like a gold digger the unique-to-you nuggets from your life.

When I was six years old, my father built us a house. *Architectural Digest* didn't notice, but my mom sure did. Dad constructed it, board by board, every day after work. My youth didn't deter him from giving me a job. He tied an empty nail apron around my waist, placed a magnet in my hands, and sent me on daily patrols around the building site, carrying my magnet only inches off the ground.

One look at my tools and you could guess my job. Stray-nail collector.

One look at yours and the same can be said. Brick by brick, life by life, God is creating a kingdom, a "spiritual house" (1 Pet. 2:5 CEV). He entrusted you with a key task in the project. Examine your tools and discover it. Your ability unveils your destiny.

When God gives an assignment, he also gives the skill. Study your skills, then, to reveal your assignment.

Look at you. Your uncanny ease with numbers. Your quenchless curiosity about chemistry. Others stare at blueprints and yawn; you read them and drool. "I was made to do this," you say.

As our Maker calls, he equips. Look back over your life. What have you consistently done well? What have you loved to do? Stand at the intersection of your affections and successes and find your uniqueness.

Cure for the Common Life

Follow Your Strengths

There are some things we want to do but simply aren't equipped to accomplish. I, for example, have the desire to sing. Singing for others would give me wonderful satisfaction. The problem is, it wouldn't give the same satisfaction to my audience. I am what you might call a prison singer—I never have the key, and I'm always behind a few bars.

Paul gives good advice in Romans 12:3: "Have a sane estimate of your capabilities" (PHILLIPS).

In other words, be aware of your strengths. When you teach, do people listen? When you lead, do people follow? When you administer, do things improve? Where are you most productive? Identify your strengths, and then—this is important—major in them. Failing to focus on our strengths may prevent us from accomplishing the unique tasks God has called us to do.

Just Like Jesus

We all have
different gifts, each of
which came because of the
grace God gave us.

ROMANS 12:6 NCV

Take a Big Risk

Use your uniqueness to take great risks for God!
If you're great with kids, volunteer at the orphanage.

If you have a head for business, start a soup kitchen.

If God bent you toward medicine, dedicate a day or a decade to AIDS patients.

The only mistake is not to risk making one. . . .

He lavished you with strengths in this life and a promise of the next. Go out on a limb; he won't let you fall. Take a big risk; he won't let you fail. He invites you to dream of the day you feel his hand on your shoulder and his eyes on your face. "Well done," he will say, "good and faithful servant."

Cure for the Common Life

God's Gallery

Do we not dwell in the gallery of our God? Isn't the sky his canvas and humanity his magnum opus? Are we not encircled by artistry? Sunsets burning. Waves billowing.

And isn't the soul his studio? The birthing of love, the bequeathing of grace. All around us miracles pop like fireflies—souls are touched, hearts are changed.

Traveling Light

Made for God's Glory

Exceptional!

Fabulous!

YOU

Original!

Unique!

Incomparable!

Wonderful!

To Reveal God's Glory

God awoke you and me this morning for one purpose: "Declare his glory among the nations, his marvelous deeds among all peoples" (1 Cor. 16:24 NIV).

"God made all things, and everything continues through him and for him. To him be the glory forever" (Rom. 11:36 NCV). "There is only one God, the Father, who created everything, and we exist for him" (1 Cor. 8:6 NLT).

Why does the earth spin? For him.
Why do you have talents and abilities? For him. . . .
Everything and everyone exists to reveal his glory.
Including you.

It's Not About Me

God's Brush Stroke

The breath you just took? God gave that. The blood that just pulsed through your heart? Credit God. The light by which you read and the brain with which you process? He gave both.

Everything comes from him . . . and exists for him. We exist to exhibit God, to display his glory. We serve as canvases for his brush stroke, papers for his pen, soil for his seeds, glimpses of his image.

Cure for the Common Life

Everything comes
from God alone. Everything
lives by his power, and
everything is for his glory.

ROMANS 11:36 TLB

Let Your Life Illustrate Christ

Tucked away in the cedar chest of my memory is the image of a robust and rather rotund children's Bible class teacher in a small West Texas church. She wore black eyeglasses that peaked on the corners like a masquerade mask. Low-heeled shoes contained her thick ankles, but nothing contained her great passion. Hugs as we entered and hugs as we left. She knew all six of us by name and made class so fun we'd rather miss the ice cream truck than Sunday school.

Here is why I tell you about her. She enjoyed giving us each a can of crayons and a sketch of Jesus torn from a coloring book. We each had our own can, mind you, reassigned from cupboard duty to classroom. What had held peaches or spinach now held a dozen or so Crayolas. "Take the crayons I gave you," she would instruct, "and color Jesus." And so we would.

We didn't illustrate pictures of ourselves; we colored the Son of God. We didn't pirate crayons from other cans; we used what she gave us. This was the fun of it.

"Do the best you can with the can you get." No blue for the sky? Make it purple. If Jesus's hair is blond instead of brown, the teacher won't mind. She loaded the can.

She taught us to paint Jesus with our own colors.

God made you to do likewise. He loaded your can. He made you unique. But knowing what he gave you is not enough. You need to understand why he gave it: so you could illustrate Christ. Make a big deal out of him. Beautify his face; adorn his image. Color Christ with the crayons God gave you.

Don't waste years embellishing your own image. No disrespect, but who needs to see your face? Who doesn't need to see God's?

Besides, God promises no applause for self-promoters. But great reward awaits God promoters: "Good work! You did your job well" (Matt. 25:23 MSG). Our teacher gave something similar. Judging by her praise, you'd think her class roll had names like Rembrandt and van Gogh. One by one she waved the just-colored Christs in the air. "Wonderful work, Max. Just wonderful!"

I smiled the size of a cantaloupe slice. You will too.

Cure for the Common Life

Use your uniqueness to make
a big deal about God.

Exhibit God

od endows us with gifts so we can make him known. Period. God endues the Olympian with speed, the salesman with savvy, the surgeon with skill. Why? For gold medals, closed sales, or healed bodies? Only partially.

The big answer is to make a big to-do out of God. Brandish him. Herald him. "God has given gifts to each of you from his great variety of spiritual gifts. Manage them well. . . . Then God will be given glory" (1 Pet. 4:10–11 NLT).

Live so that "he'll get all the credit as the One mighty in everything—encores to the end of time. Oh, yes!" (1 Pet. 4:11 MSG). Exhibit God with your uniqueness. When you magnify your Maker with your strengths, when your contribution enriches God's reputation, your days grow suddenly sweet.

Cure for the Common Life

The Highest Purpose

Why did God pack your life as he did?

Accountant, how do you explain your number sense?

Investor, you read the stock market like Bobby Fischer reads the chessboard. Ever wondered why you have such a skill?

Linguist, foreign languages paralyze most tongues, but they liberate yours. Why?

And, homemaker, you make your household purr like a Rolls-Royce. For what purpose?

So people will love you? Pay you? Admire you? Hire you? If your answer involves only you, you've missed the big reason, and you're making the big mistake.

Use your best gifts to serve the highest purpose: making a big deal out of God.

Cure for the Common Life

YOU **God's Brand-New Idea**

What talents has God packed into your life?

I will extol You,

O LORD, for

You have lifted me up.

PSALM 30:1 NKJV

With God in Mind

Michelangelo was born to sculpt. He once commented that he could taste the tools of a stonecutter in the milk of his wet nurse. He'd sculpted a mature work by the age of twenty-one. By the age of thirty he had produced the still-stunning masterpieces Pietà and David.

When Michelangelo was in his early thirties, the pope invited him to Rome to complete a special project. Pope Julius II initially asked him to sculpt a papal tomb but then changed his plans and invited him to paint a dozen figures on the ceiling of a Vatican chapel. The sculptor was tempted to refuse. Painting was not his first passion, and a small chapel was not his idea of a great venue. But the pope urged him to accept, so he did. Some historians suspect a setup. Jealous contemporaries convinced the pope to issue the invitation, certain the sculptor would decline and fall into the disfavor of the pontiff.

Michelangelo didn't decline. He began the work. And as he painted, his enthusiasm mounted. Four years, four hundred figures, and nine scenes later, Michelangelo had changed more than the chapel; he'd changed the direction of art. His bold frescoes rerouted the style of European painting. He so immersed himself in the project that he nearly lost his health. "I felt as old and as weary as Jeremiah," he said of his state. "I was only thirty-seven, yet my friends did not recognize the old man I had become."

What happened? What changed him? What turned his work of obligation into an act of inspiration? The answer might lie in a response he gave to a question. An observer wondered why he focused such attention on the details of the corners of the chapel. "No one will ever see them," he suggested.

Michelangelo's reply? "God will."

The artist must have known this passage: "Work with enthusiasm, as though you were working for the Lord rather than for people" (Eph. 6:7 NLT).

God's cure for the common life includes a change in our reporting lines. May I remind you that we have two bosses: one who signs our checks and one who saves our souls. The second has keen interest in our workaday world. What if everyone worked with God in mind?

Cure for the Common Life
YOU **God's Brand-New Idea**

If we boast at all,
we "boast in the Lord."

2 CORINTHIANS 10:17 NASB

Lift Up Your Gift

God has never taken his eyes off you. Not for a millisecond. He's always near. He lives to hear your heartbeat. He loves to hear your prayers. He'd die for your sin before he'd let you die in your sin, so he did.

What do you do with such a Savior? Don't you sing to him? Don't you declare, confess, and proclaim his name? Don't you bow a knee, lower a head, hammer a nail, feed the poor, and lift up your gift in worship? Of course you do.

Worship God. Applaud him loud and often. For your sake, you need it.

And for heaven's sake, he deserves it.

Cure for the Common Life

Since you are
God's idea,

you are a good idea.

Made for God's Plan

God's Plan for Your Life

God's plan for you is nothing short of a new heart. If you were a car, God would want control of your engine. If you were a computer, God would claim the software and the hard drive. If you were an airplane, he'd take his seat in the cockpit. But you are a person, so God wants to change your heart.

God wants you to be just like Jesus. He wants you to have a heart like his.

It's dangerous to sum up grand truths in one statement, but I'm going to try. If a sentence or two could capture God's desire for each of us, it might read like this: God loves you just the way you are, but he refuses to leave you that way. He wants you to be just like Jesus.

God loves you just the way you are. If you think his love for you would be stronger if your faith were, you are wrong. If you think his love would be deeper if your thoughts were, wrong again. Don't confuse God's love with the love of people. The love of people often increases with performance and decreases with mistakes. Not so with God's love. He loves you right where you are. He loves you just the way you are, but he refuses to leave you that way.

Just Like Jesus

YOU **God's Brand-New Idea**

—— 101 ——

Total Transformation

G od has ambitious plans for us. The same one who saved your soul longs to remake your heart. His plan is nothing short of a total transformation: "He decided from the outset to shape the lives of those who love him along the same lines as the life of his Son."

God wants you to fly. He wants you to fly free of yesterday's guilt. He wants you to fly free of today's fears. He wants you to fly free of tomorrow's grave. Sin, fear, and death. These are the mountains he has moved. These are the prayers he will answer. That is the fruit he will grant. This is what he longs to do.

And the Angels Were Silent

How can you use your talents for God's purpose?

"Before I made you
in your mother's womb,
I chose you."

JEREMIAH 1:5 NCV

Serving Uniquely

When we submit to God's plans, we can trust our desires. Our assignment is found at the intersection of God's plan and our pleasures. *What do you love to do? What brings you joy? What gives you a sense of satisfaction?*

Some long to feed the poor. Others enjoy leading the church. Others relish singing or teaching or holding the hands of the sick or counseling the confused. Each of us has been made to serve God in a unique way.

Just Like Jesus

Collectively, We Inspire

Scripture calls the church a poem. "We are His workmanship" (Eph. 2:10 NKJV). *Workmanship* descends from the Greek word *poeo* or *poetry*. We are God's poetry! What Longfellow did with pen and paper, our Maker does with us. We express his creative best.

You aren't God's poetry. I'm not God's poetry. *We* are God's poetry. Poetry demands variety. "God works through different men in different ways, but it is the same God who achieves his purposes through them all" (1 Cor. 12:6 PHILLIPS). God uses all types to type his message. Logical thinkers. Emotional worshipers. Dynamic leaders. Docile followers. The visionaries who lead, the studious who ponder, the generous who pay the bills. . . . Alone, we are meaningless symbols on a page. But collectively, we inspire.

Cure for the Common Life

God Knows You by Name

When I see a flock of sheep I see exactly that, a flock. A rabble of wool. A herd of hooves. I don't see a sheep. I see sheep. All alike. None different. That's what I see.

But not so with the shepherd. To him every sheep is different. Every face is special. Every face has a story. And every sheep has a name. *The one with the sad eyes, that's Droopy. And the fellow with one ear up and the other down, I call him Oscar. And the small one with the black patch on his leg, he's an orphan with no brothers. I call him Joseph.*

The shepherd knows his sheep. He calls them by name. When we see a crowd, we see exactly that, a crowd. Filling a stadium or flooding a mall. When we see a crowd, we see people, not persons, but people. A herd of humans. A flock of faces. That's what we see.

But not so with the Shepherd. To him every face is different. Every face is a story. Every face is a child. Every child has a name. *The one with the sad eyes, that's Sally. The old fellow with one eyebrow up and the other down, Harry's his name. And the young one with the limp? He's an orphan with no brothers. I call him Joey.*

The Shepherd knows his sheep. He knows each one by name. The Shepherd knows you. He knows your name. And he will never forget it. *"I have written your name on my hand"* (Isa. 49:16 NCV).

Quite a thought, isn't it? Your name on God's hand. Your name on God's lips. Maybe you've seen your name in some special places. On an award or diploma or walnut door. Or maybe you've heard your name from some important people—a coach, a celebrity, a teacher. But to think that your name is on God's hand and on God's lips . . . my, could it be?

Written on his hand. Spoken by his mouth. Whispered by his lips. Your name.

When God Whispers Your Name

The Shepherd

knows your name.

When our gifts
illuminate God and
help his children,
don't you think he beams!

He will rejoice over you.
You will rest in
his love; he will sing and
be joyful about you.

ZEPHANIAH 3:17 NKJV

The God-Centered Life

The moon generates no light. Contrary to the lyrics of the song, this harvest moon cannot shine on. Apart from the sun, the moon is nothing more than a pitch-black, pockmarked rock. But properly positioned, the moon beams. Let her do what she was made to do, and a clod of dirt becomes a source of inspiration, yea, verily, romance. The moon reflects the greater light.

And she's happy to do so! You never hear the moon complaining. She makes no waves about making waves. Let the cow jump over her or astronauts step on her; she never objects. . . .

The moon is at peace in her place. And because she is, soft light touches a dark earth. . . .

What would happen if we took our places and played our parts? If we played the music the Maestro gave us to play? If we made his song our highest priority?

Talk about a Copernican shift. Talk about a healthy shift. Life makes sense when we accept our place. The gift of pleasure, the purpose of problems—all for him. The God-centered life works. And it rescues us from a life that doesn't.

It's Not About Me

It is no longer I who live,
but Christ lives in me.

GALATIANS 2:20 NASB

Christ Within

What would it be like? To have Christ within?

To have my voice, but him speaking.
My steps, but Christ leading.
My heart, but his love beating
in me, through me, with me.
What's it like to have Christ on the inside?

To tap his strength when mine expires
or feel the force of heaven's fires
raging, purging wrong desires.
Could Christ become my self entire?

So much him, so little me
that in my eyes it's him they see.
No longer I, but Christ in me.

Next Door Savior

A Sleek Racing Machine

In high school my brother and I shared a '65 Rambler station wagon. The clunker had as much glamour as Forrest Gump: three speed, shift on the column, bench seats covered with plastic, no air conditioning.

And, oh, the engine. Our lawn mower had more power. The car's highest speed, downhill with a tailwind, was fifty miles per hour. To this day I'm convinced that my father (a trained mechanic) searched for the slowest possible car and bought it for us.

When we complained about her pitiful shape, he just smiled and said, "Fix it up." We did the best we could. We cleaned the carpets, sprayed air freshener on the seats, stuck a peace symbol on the back window, and hung Styrofoam dice from the rearview mirror. We removed the hubcaps and spray-painted the rims black. The car looked better, smelled better, but ran the same. Still a clunker—a clean clunker, to be sure—but still a clunker.

Don't for a microsecond think God does this with you. Washing the outside isn't enough for him. He places power on the inside. Better stated, he places himself on the inside.

When you believe in Christ, Christ works a miracle in you. "When you believed in Christ, he identified you as his own by giving you the Holy Spirit" (Eph. 1:13 NLT). You are permanently  purified and empowered by God himself. The message of Jesus . . . is simple: It's not what you do. It's what I do. I have moved in. And in time you can say with Paul, "I myself no longer live, but Christ lives in me" (Gal. 2:20 NLT). You are no longer a clunker, not even a clean clunker. You are a sleek Indianapolis Motor Speedway racing machine.

Next Door Savior

God Is Cheering You

G od *is* for you. Not "may be," not "has been," not "was," not "would be," but "God is!" He *is* for you. Today. At this hour. At this minute. As you read this sentence. No need to wait in line or come back tomorrow. He is with you.

God is *for* you. Turn to the sidelines; that's God cheering your run. Look past the finish line; that's God applauding your steps. Listen for him in the bleachers, shouting your name. Too tired to continue? He'll carry you. Too discouraged to fight? He's picking you up. God is for you.

God is for *you*. Had he a calendar, your birthday would be circled. If he drove a car, your name would be on his bumper. If there's a tree in heaven, he's carved your name in the bark. We know he has a tattoo, and we know what it says. "I have written your name on my hand." (Isa. 49:16 NCV).

In the Grip of Grace

Use Your Uniqueness

You have one. A divine spark. An uncommon call to an uncommon life. "The Spirit has given each of us a *special way* of serving others" (1 Cor. 2:7 CEV). So much for the excuse "I don't have anything to offer." Did the apostle Paul say, "The Spirit has given *some* of us . . ."? Or, "The Spirit has given *a few* of us . . . "? No. "The Spirit has given *each of us* a special way of serving others." Enough of this self-deprecating "I can't do anything."

And enough of its arrogant opposite: "I have to do everything." No, you don't! You're not God's solution to society, but a solution in society. Imitate Paul, who said, "Our goal is to stay within the boundaries of God's plan for us" (2 Cor. 10:13 NLT). Clarify your contribution.

Don't worry about skills you don't have. Don't covet strengths others do have. Just extract your uniqueness.

Cure for the Common Life

Made to Be Loved by God

The LORD

loves you.

DEUTERONOMY 7:8 NLT

You Are Loved by God

God loves you simply because he has chosen to do so.

He loves you when you don't feel lovely.

He loves you when no one else loves you. Others may abandon you, divorce you, and ignore you, but God will love you. Always. No matter what.

This is his sentiment: "I'll call nobodies and make them somebodies; I'll call the unloved and make them beloved" (Rom. 9:25 MSG).

This is his promise. "I have loved you, my people, with an everlasting love. With unfailing love I have drawn you to myself" (Jer. 31:3 NLT).

A Love Worth Giving

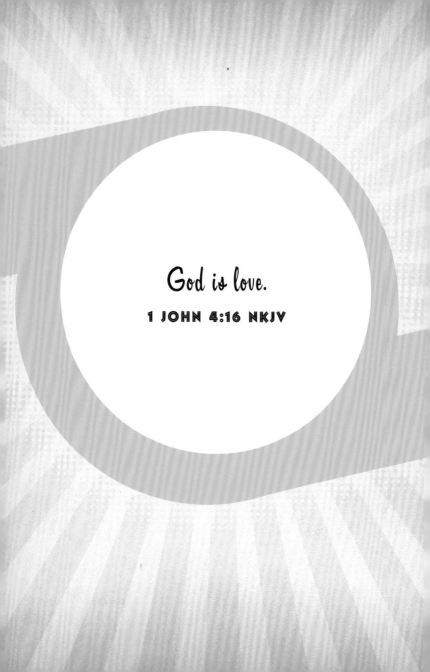

God is love.

1 JOHN 4:16 NKJV

The Surprise of God's Love

The supreme surprise of God's love? It has nothing to do with you. Others love you because of you, because your dimples dip when you smile or your rhetoric charms when you flirt. Some people love you because of you. Not God. He loves you because he is he. He loves you because he decides to. Self-generated, uncaused, and spontaneous, his constant-level love depends on his choice to give it. "The LORD did not set his affection on you and choose you because you were more numerous than other peoples, for you were the fewest of all peoples. But it was because the LORD loved you" (Deut. 7:7–8 NIV).

You don't influence God's love. You can't impact the treeness of a tree, the skyness of the sky, or the rockness of a rock. Nor can you affect the love of God.

Come Thirsty

Our Value Is Inborn

In God's book man is heading somewhere. He has an amazing destiny. We are being prepared to walk down the church aisle and become the bride of Jesus. We are going to live with him. Share the throne with him. Reign with him. We count. We are valuable. And what's more, our worth is built in! Our value is inborn.

You see, if there was anything that Jesus wanted everyone to understand it was this: A person is worth something simply because he is a person. That is why he treated people like he did. . . .

Listen closely. Jesus' love does not depend upon what we do for him. Not at all. In the eyes of the King, you have value simply because you *are*. You don't have to look nice or perform well. Your value is inborn.

Period.

Think about that for just a minute. You are valuable just because you exist. Not because of what you do or what you have done, but simply because you are.

No Wonder They Call Him the Savior

I have loved you with an everlasting love.

MALACHI 1:2 NKJV

Let God have you,
let God love you.

What About Love?

The love of a parent for a child is a mighty force. Consider the couple with their newborn child. The infant offers his parents absolutely nothing. No money. No skill. No words of wisdom. If he had pockets, they would be empty. To see an infant lying in a bassinet is to see utter helplessness. What is there to love?

Whatever it is, Mom and Dad find it. Just look at Mom's face as she nurses her baby. Just watch Dad's eyes as he cradles the child. And just try to harm or speak evil of the infant. If you do, you'll encounter a mighty strength, for the love of a parent is a mighty force.

Jesus once asked, if we humans who are sinful have such a love, how much more does God, the sinless and selfless Father, love us? (Matt. 7:11)

He Chose the Nails

How Wide Is God's Love?

For God so loved the world that he gave his only
Son" (John 3:16 NLT).

As boldly as the center beam of the cross proclaims
God's holiness, the crossbeam declares his love. And, oh,
how wide his love reaches.

Aren't you glad the verse does not read:

"For God so loved the rich . . ."?

Or, "For God so loved the famous . . ."?

Or, "For God so loved the thin . . ."?

It doesn't. Nor does it state, "For God so loved the Europeans or Africans . . . " "the sober or successful . . . " "the young or the old . . . "

No, when we read John 3:16, we simply (and happily) read, "For God so loved the world."

How wide is God's love? Wide enough for the whole world.

He Chose the Nails

YOU **God's Brand-New Idea**

You Are Included

It's nice to be included. You aren't always. Universities exclude you if you aren't smart enough. Businesses exclude you if you aren't qualified enough, and, sadly, some churches exclude you if you aren't good enough.

But though they may exclude you, Christ includes you. When asked to describe the width of his love, he stretched one hand to the right and the other to the left and had them nailed in that position so you would know he died loving you.

But isn't there a limit? Surely there has to be an end to this love. You'd think so, wouldn't you? But David the adulterer never found it. Paul the murderer never found it. Peter the liar never found it. When it came to life, they hit bottom. But when it came to God's love, they never did.

He Chose the Nails

Such a Gift!

Who has plumbed the depths of God's love? Only God has. "Want to see the size of my love?" he invites. "Ascend the winding path outside of Jerusalem. Follow the dots of bloody dirt until you crest the hill. Before looking up, pause and hear me whisper, "This is how much I love you." . . .

Does God love you? Behold the cross, and behold your answer.

God the Son died for you. Who could have imagined such a gift?

It's Not About Me

When it comes to God's love,
we will never find the limit.

God's Perfect Love

We all need improvement, but we don't need to woo God's love. We change because we already have God's love. God's perfect love.

Perfect love is just that—perfect, a perfect knowledge of the past and a perfect vision of the future. You cannot shock God with your actions. There will never be a day that you cause him to gasp, "Whoa, did you see what she just did?" Never will he turn to his angels and bemoan, "Had I known Max was going to go Spambrained on me, I wouldn't have saved his soul." God knows your entire story, from first word to final breath, and with clear assessment declares, "You are mine."

My publisher made a similar decision with this book. Before agreeing to publish it, they read it—every single word. Multiple sets of editorial eyes scoured the manuscript, moaning at my bad jokes, grading my word crafting, suggesting a tune-up here and a tone-down there. We volleyed pages back and forth, writer to editor to writer, until finally we all agreed—this is it. It's time to publish or pass. The publisher could pass, mind you. Sometimes they do. But in this case, obviously they didn't. With perfect knowledge of this imperfect product, they signed on. What you read may surprise you, but not them.

What you do may stun you, but not God. With perfect knowledge of your imperfect life, God signed on.

Come Thirsty

Exceptional!

Fabulous!

Original!

Unique!

Incomparable!

Wonderful!

God Knows You

God knows you. And he is near you! How far is the shepherd from the sheep (John 10:14)? The branch from the vine (John 15:5)? That's how far God is from you. He is near. See how these four words look taped to your bathroom mirror: "God is for me" (Ps. 56:9 NKJV).

And his kingdom needs you. The poor need you; the lonely need you; the church needs you . . . the cause of God needs you. You are part of "the overall purpose he is working out in everything and everyone" (Eph. 1:11 MSG). The kingdom needs you to discover and deploy your unique skill. Use it to make much out of God. Get the word out. God is with us; we are not alone.

Cure for the Common Life

eaven never exports monotony. Christ once announced: "I came so they can have real and eternal life, more and better life than they ever dreamed of" (John 10:10 MSG). Nor does God author loneliness. Among our Maker's first recorded words were these: "It is not good for the man to be alone" (Gen. 2:18 NIV).

He gets no argument from us. We may relish moments of solitude—but a lifetime of it? No way.

Ever since Eve emerged from the bone of Adam, we've been reaching out to touch one another. We need to make a connection. And we need to make a difference.

Remember the promise of the angel? "'Behold, the virgin shall be with child, and bear a Son, and they shall call His name Immanuel,' which is translated, 'God with us'" (Matt. 1:23).

Immanuel. The name appears in the same Hebrew form as it did two thousand years ago. "Immanu" means "with us." "El" refers to Elohim, or God. Not an "above us God" or a "somewhere in the neighborhood God." He came as the "with us God." God with us.

God *with* us. Don't we love the word "with"? "Will you go *with* me?" we ask. "To the store, to the hospital, through my life?" God says he will. "I am *with* you always," Jesus said before he ascended to heaven, "to the very end of the age" (Matt. 28:20 NIV). Search for restrictions on the promise; you'll find none. You won't find "I'll be with you if you behave . . . when you believe. I'll be with you on Sundays in worship . . . at mass." No, none of that. There's no withholding tax on God's "with" promise. He is *with* us.

Cure for the Common Life

God's love supply is never empty. "For his unfailing love toward those who fear him is as great as the height of the heavens above the earth" (Ps. 103:11 NLT).

The big news of the Bible is not that you love God but that God loves you; not that you can know God but that God already knows you! He tattooed your name on the palm of his hand. His thoughts of you outnumber the sand on the shore. You never leave his mind, escape his sight, flee his thoughts. He sees the worst of you and loves you still. Your sins of tomorrow and failings of the future will not surprise him; he sees them now. Every day and deed of your life has passed before his eyes and been calculated in his decision. He knows you better than you know you and has reached his verdict: he loves you still. No discovery will disillusion him; no rebellion will dissuade him. He loves you with an everlasting love.

Come Thirsty

YOU **God's Brand-New Idea**

You have never lived
a loveless day. Not one.

God's Love Filters Your Life

Every so often in life, we find ourselves standing before God's counter, thinking we know the itinerary. Good health, a job promotion, a pregnancy. Many times God checks the itinerary he created and says yes. But there are times when he says, "No. That isn't the journey I have planned for you. I have you routed through the city of Struggle."

We can stamp our feet and shake our fists. Or we can make a sailor-in-the-storm decision. *I know God knows what is best.*

He authors all itineraries. He knows what is best. No struggle will come your way apart from his purpose, presence, and permission. What encouragement this brings! You are never the victim of nature or the prey of fate. Chance is eliminated. You are more than a weather vane whipped about by the winds of fortune.

We live beneath the protective palm of a sovereign King who superintends every circumstance of our lives and delights in doing us good.

Nothing comes your way that has not first passed through the filter of his love.

Learn well the song of sovereignty: *I know God knows what's best.* Pray humbly the prayer of trust: "I trust your lordship. I belong to you. Nothing comes to me that hasn't passed through you."

And be encouraged. God's ways are always right. They may not make sense to us. They may be mysterious, inexplicable, difficult, and even painful. But they are right. "And we know that God causes everything to work together for the good of those who love God and are called according to his purpose for them" (Rom. 8:28 NLT).

Come Thirsty

Made to Love God

Delivering Christ to the World

G od grants us an uncommon life to the degree we surrender our common one. "If you try to keep your life for yourself, you will lose it. But if you give up your life for me, you will find true life" (Matt. 16:25 NLT). Would you forfeit your reputation to see Jesus born into your world?

Jesus "made Himself of no reputation, taking the form of a bondservant, and coming in the likeness of men. And being found in appearance as a man, He humbled Himself and became obedient to the point of death, even the death of the cross" (Phil. 2:7–8 NKJV).

Christ abandoned his reputation. No one in Nazareth saluted him as the Son of God. He did not stand out in his elementary-classroom photograph, demanded no glossy page in his high school annual. Friends knew him as a woodworker, not star hanger. His looks turned no heads; his position earned him no credit. In the great stoop we call Christmas, Jesus abandoned heavenly privileges and aproned earthly pains. "He gave up his place with God and made himself nothing" (Phil. 2:7 NCV).

God hunts for those who will do likewise—people through whom he can deliver Christ into the world.

Cure for the Common Life

God designed and gave you
a unique mix of strengths so
you can accomplish the special purpose
he has in mind for you.
As you understand your giftedness,
you can build your future
around it.

What a Man Sees

Should a man see only popularity, he becomes a mirror, reflecting whatever needs to be reflected to gain acceptance.

Should a man see only power, he becomes a wolf—prowling, hunting, and stalking the elusive game. Recognition is his prey and people are his prizes. His quest is endless.

Should a man see only pleasure, he becomes a carnival thrill-seeker, alive only in bright lights, wild rides, and titillating entertainment.

Only in seeing his Maker does a man truly become man. For in seeing his Creator, man catches a glimpse of what he was intended to be.

God Came Near

Human life comes from human parents, but spiritual life comes from the Spirit.

JOHN 3:6 NCV

Spiritual life comes from the Spirit! Your parents may have given you genes, but God gives you grace. Your parents may be responsible for your body, but God has taken charge of your soul. You may get your looks from your mother, but you get eternity from your Father, your heavenly Father.

When God Whispers Your Name

Full of Yourself?

When you're full of yourself, God can't fill you. But when you empty yourself, God has a useful vessel. Your Bible overflows with examples of those who did.

In his gospel, Matthew mentions his own name only twice. Both times he calls himself a tax collector. In his list of apostles, he assigns himself the eighth spot.

John doesn't even mention his name in his gospel. The twenty appearances of "John" all refer to the Baptist. John the apostle simply calls himself "the other disciple" or the "disciple whom Jesus loved."

Luke wrote two of the most important books in the Bible but never once penned his own name.

Paul, the Bible's most prolific author, referred to himself as "a fool" (2 Cor. 12:11 NKJV). He also called himself the "least of the apostles" (1 Cor. 15:9 NKJV).

King David wrote no psalm celebrating his victory over Goliath. But he wrote a public poem of penitence confessing his sin with Bathsheba (see Ps. 51).

And then there is Joseph. The quiet father of Jesus. Rather than make a name for himself, he made a home for Christ. And because he did, a great reward came his way. "He called His name Jesus" (Matt. 1:25 NKJV).

Cure for the Common Life

We are ambassadors for Christ, as though God were making an appeal through us" (2 Cor. 5:20 NASB). The ambassador has a singular aim—to represent his king. He promotes the king's agenda, protects the king's reputation, and presents the king's will. The ambassador elevates the name of the king.

May I add a prayer that we do the same?

It's Not About Me

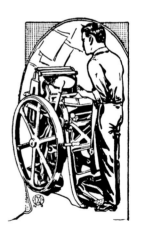

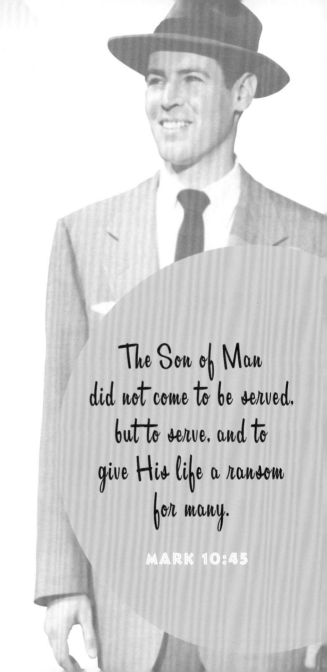

The Son of Man
did not come to be served,
but to serve, and to
give His life a ransom
for many.

MARK 10:45

When your deepest
desire is not
the things of God,
or a favor from God,
but God himself,
you cross a threshold.

Make a Big Deal About God

There are two extremes of poor I-sight. Self-loving and self-loathing. We swing from one side to the other. Promotions and demotions bump us back and forth. One day too high on self, the next too hard on self. Neither is correct. Self-elevation and self-deprecation are equally inaccurate. Where is the truth?

Smack-dab in the middle. Dead center between "I can do anything" and "I can't do anything" lies "I can do all things through Christ who strengthens me" (Phil. 4:13).

Neither omnipotent nor impotent, neither God's MVP nor God's mistake. Not self-secure or insecure, but God-secure—a self-worth based in our identity as children of God. The proper view of self is in the middle.

But how do we get there? How do we park the pendulum in the center? Counseling? Therapy? Self-help? Long walks? Taking Lucado out to dinner? Advisable activities, but they don't compare with God's cure for poor I-sight:

Worship.

Surprised? The word conjures up many thoughts, not all of which are positive. Outdated songs. Cliché-cluttered prayers. Irrelevant sermons. Meager offerings. Odd rituals. Why worship? What does worship have to do with curing the common life?

Honest worship lifts eyes off self and sets them on God. Scripture's best-known worship leader wrote: "Give honor to the LORD, you angels; give honor to the LORD for his glory and strength. Give honor to the LORD for the glory of his name. Worship the LORD in the splendor of his holiness" (Ps. 29:1–2 NLT).

Worship gives God honor, offers him standing ovations.

We can make a big deal about God on Sundays with our songs and on Mondays with our strengths. Every day in every deed. Each time we do our best to thank God for giving his, we worship. "Take your everyday, ordinary life—your sleeping, eating, going-to-work, and walking-around life—and place it before God as an offering" (Rom. 12:1 MSG). Worship places God on center stage and us in proper posture.

Cure for the Common Life

Exceptional!

Fabulous!

Original!

Unique!

Incomparable!

Wonderful!

hey did not conquer the land with their swords; it was not their own strength that gave them victory. It was by your mighty power that they succeeded; it was because you favored them and smiled on them" (Ps. 44:3 NLT).

I know a frog who needed those verses. He had a real problem. His home pond was drying up. If he didn't find water soon, he would do the same. Word reached him of a vibrant stream over the adjacent hill. If only he could live there. But how could he? The short legs of a frog were not made for long journeys.

But then he had an idea. Convincing two birds to carry either end of a stick, he bit the center and held on as they flew. As they winged toward the new water, his jaws were clamped tightly. It was quite a sight! Two birds, one stick, and a frog in the middle. Down below, a cow in a pasture saw them passing overhead. Impressed, he wondered aloud, "Now who came up with that idea?"

The frog overheard his question and couldn't resist a reply. "I diiiiiii . . ."

Don't make the same mistake. "Pride goes before destruction, and haughtiness before a fall" (Prov. 16:18 NLT). Why are you good at what you do? For your comfort? For your self-esteem? No. Deem these as bonuses, not as the reason. Why are you good at what you do? For God's sake. Your success is not about what you do. It's all about him—his present and future glory.

It's Not About Me

Christianity, in its purest form,
is nothing more than
seeing Jesus.

Christian service, in its purest form,
is nothing more than
imitating him who we see.

A Message from God

* I throw my arms around you, lavish attention on you, and guard you as the apple of my eye.
* I rejoice over you with great gladness.
* My thoughts of you cannot be counted: they outnumber the grains of sand!
* Nothing can ever separate you from my love. Death can't, and life can't. The angels can't, and the demons can't. Your fears for today, your worries about tomorrow, and even the powers of hell can't keep my love away.

(Deut. 32:10 MSG: Zeph. 3:17 NLT:
Psalm 139:17–18 NLT: Rom. 8:38 NLT)

A Life of Popularity?

God's cure for the common life includes a strong dose of servanthood. Timely reminder. As you celebrate your unique design, be careful. Don't so focus on what you love to do that you neglect what needs to be done. . . .

The world needs servants. People like Jesus who "did not come to be served, but to serve." He chose remote Nazareth over center-stage Jerusalem, his dad's carpentry shop over a marble-columned palace, and three decades of anonymity over a life of popularity.

Jesus came to serve. He selected prayer over sleep, the wilderness over the Jordan, irascible apostles over obedient angels. I'd have gone with the angels. Given the choice, I would have built my apostle team out of cherubim and seraphim or Gabriel and Michael, eyewitnesses of Red Sea rescues and Mount Carmel falling fires. I'd choose the angels.

Not Jesus. He picked the people. Peter, Andrew, John, and Matthew. When they feared the storm, he stilled it.

When they had no coin for taxes, he supplied it. And when they had no wine for the wedding or food for the multitude, he made both.

He came to serve.

He let a woman in Samaria interrupt his rest, a woman in adultery interrupt his sermon, a woman with a disease interrupt his plans, and one with remorse interrupt his meal.

Though none of the apostles washed his feet, he washed theirs. Though none of the soldiers at the cross begged for mercy, he extended it. And though his followers skedaddled like scared rabbits on Thursday, he came searching for them on Easter Sunday. The resurrected King ascended to heaven only after he'd spent forty days with his friends—teaching them, encouraging them . . . serving them.

Why? It's what he came to do. He came to serve.

Cure for the Common Life

A Listening Heart

Listening to God is a firsthand experience. When he asks for your attention, God doesn't want you to send a substitute; he wants you. He wants to spend time with you.

Equipped with the right tools, we can learn to listen to God. What are those tools? Here are the ones I have found helpful.

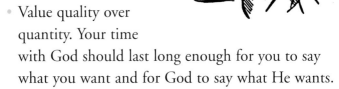

- A regular time and place. Select a slot on your schedule and a corner of your world, and claim it for God.
- Value quality over quantity. Your time with God should last long enough for you to say what you want and for God to say what He wants.

- Another tool you need is *an open Bible*. The first step in reading the Bible is to ask God to help you understand it.
- Before reading the Bible, pray. Don't go to Scripture looking for your own idea; go searching for God's.
- Study the Bible a little at a time. Choose depth over quantity.
- Not only do we need a regular time and an open Bible, we also need a *listening heart*. Spend time listening for God until you receive your lesson for the day—then apply it.

We know we are listening to God when what we read in the Bible is what others see in our lives.

Just Like Jesus

Each time we do our best to thank
God for giving his. we worship.

God Is Kind to You

Our heavenly Father is kind to us. And since he is so kind to us, can't we be a little kinder to ourselves? *Oh, but you don't know me, Max. You don't know my faults and my thoughts. You don't know the gripes I grumble and the complaints I mumble.* No, I don't, but he does. He knows everything about you, yet he doesn't hold back his kindness toward you. Has he, knowing all your secrets, retracted one promise or reclaimed one gift?

No, he is kind to you. Why don't you be kind to yourself? He forgives your faults. Why don't you do the same? He thinks tomorrow is worth living. Why don't you agree? He believes in you enough to call you his ambassador, his follower, even his child. Why not take his cue and believe in yourself?

A Love Worth Giving

Our Work Matters

> [Jesus] climbed into the boat that was
> [Peter's] and asked him to put out a little
> from the shore. Sitting there, using the boat
> for a pulpit, he taught the crowd
> (Luke 5:2–3 MSG).

Jesus claims Peter's boat. He doesn't *request* the use of it. Christ doesn't fill out an application or ask permission; he simply boards the boat and begins to preach.

He can do that, you know. All boats belong to Christ. Your boat is where you spend your day, make your living, and to a large degree live your life. The taxi you drive, the horse stable you clean, the dental office you manage, the family you feed and transport—this is your boat. Christ shoulder-taps us and reminds:

"You drive my truck."

"You preside in my courtroom."

"You work on my job site."

"You serve my hospital wing."

To us all, Jesus says, "Your work is my work."

Have you seen the painting *The Angelus* by Jean-Francois Millet? It portrays two peasants praying in their field. A church steeple sits on the horizon, and a light falls from heaven. The rays do not fall on the church, however. They don't fall on the bowed heads of the man and woman. The rays of the sun fall on the wheelbarrow and the pitchfork at the couple's feet.

God's eyes fall on the work of our hands. Our Wednesdays matter to him as much as our Sundays. He blurs the secular and sacred. One stay-at-home mom keeps this sign over her kitchen sink: Divine tasks performed here, daily. An executive hung this plaque in her office: My desk is my altar. Both are correct. With God, our work matters as much as our worship. Indeed, work can be worship.

Peter, the boat owner, later wrote: "You are a chosen people. You are a kingdom of priests, God's holy nation, his very own possession. This is so you can show others the goodness of God" (1 Pet. 2:9 NLT).

Next time a job application requests your prior employment, write "priest" or "priestess," for you are one. A priest represents God, and you, my friend, represent God. So "let every detail in your lives—words, actions, whatever—be done in the name of the Master, Jesus" (Col. 3:17 MSG). You don't drive to an office; you drive to a sanctuary. You don't attend a school; you attend a temple. You may not wear a clerical collar, but you could. Your boat is God's pulpit.

Cure for the Common Life

YOU **God's Brand-New Idea**

God wants to be as close to us as a branch is to a vine. One is an extension of the other. It's impossible to tell where one starts and the other ends.

You Get to Choose

Jesus gives the invitation. "Here I am! I stand at the door and knock" (Rev. 3:20 NCV). To know God is to receive his invitation. Not just to hear it . . . but to receive it.

His invitation is clear and nonnegotiable. He gives all and we give him all. Simple and absolute. He is clear in what he asks and clear in what he offers. The choice is up to us.

Isn't it incredible that God leaves the choice to us? Think about it. There are many things in life we can't choose. We can't, for example, choose the weather. We can't control the economy.

We can't choose whether or not we are born with a big nose or blue eyes or a lot of hair. We can't even choose how people respond to us.

But we can choose where we spend eternity. The big choice, God leaves to us.

And the Angels Were Silent

God Invites Us to Love Him

We are free either to love God or not. He invites us to love him. He urges us to love him. He came that we might love him. But, in the end, the choice is yours and mine. To take that choice from each of us, for him to force us to love him, would be less than love.

God explains the benefits, outlines the promises, and articulates very clearly the consequences. And then, in the end, he leaves the choice to us.

And the Angels Were Silent

We exist to give honor
to God's name.

An Amazing Life Begins with God

It makes no sense to seek your God-given strength until you trust in his. "It's in Christ that we find out who we are and what we are living for" (Eph. 1:11 MSG). Take a few moments and talk to God. Whether you are making a decision or reaffirming an earlier one, talk to your Maker about your eternal life. You might find this prayer helpful: *Immanuel, you are with me. You became a person and took on flesh. You became a Savior and took on my sin. I accept your gift. I receive you as my Lord, Savior, and friend. Because of you, I'll never be alone again.*

Recently, the bank sent me an overdraft notice on the checking account of one of my daughters. I encourage my college-age girls to monitor their accounts. Even so, they sometimes overspend.

What should I do? Let the bank absorb it? They won't. Send her an angry letter? Admonition might help her later, but it won't satisfy the bank. Phone and tell her to make a deposit? Might as well tell a fish to fly. I know her liquidity. Zero.

Transfer the money from my account to hers? Seemed to be the best option. After all, I had $25.37. I could replenish her account and pay the overdraft fee as well.

Besides, that's my job. Don't get any ideas. If you're overdrawn, don't call me. My daughter can do something you can't do: she can call me Dad. And since she calls me Dad, I did what dads do. I covered my daughter's mistake.

When I told her she was overdrawn, she said she was sorry. Still, she offered no deposit. She was broke. She had one option. "Dad, could you . . . " I interrupted her sentence.

"Honey, I already have." I met her need before she knew she had one.

Long before you knew you needed grace, your Father did the same. He made the deposit, an ample deposit. "Christ died for us while we were still sinners"

(Rom. 5:8 NCV). Before you knew you needed a Savior, you had one. And when you ask him for mercy, he answers, "I've already given it, dear child. I've already given it."

And there's more! When you place your trust in Christ, he places his Spirit in you. And when the Spirit comes, he brings gifts, housewarming gifts of sorts. "A spiritual gift is given to each of us as a means of helping the entire church" (1 Cor. 12:7 NLT). Remember, God prepacked you with strengths. When you become a child of God, the Holy Spirit requisitions your abilities for the expansion of God's kingdom, and they become spiritual gifts. The Holy Spirit may add other gifts according to his plan. But no one is gift deprived.

An amazing life begins and ends with God.

Cure for the Common Life

What are some of the things you dream about doing for God?

Fix Your Life on Jesus

To be just like Jesus. The world has never known a heart so pure, a character so flawless. His spiritual hearing was so keen he never missed a heavenly whisper. His mercy so abundant he never missed a chance to forgive. No lie left his lips, no distraction marred his vision. He touched when others recoiled. He endured when others quit. Jesus is the ultimate model for every person. . . .

God urges you to fix your eyes upon Jesus. Heaven invites you to set the lens of your heart on the heart of the Savior and make him the object of your life.

Just Like Jesus

God knows your
beginning and
your end, because
he has neither.

"Write carefully."

Each Life Is a Book

The Author sees them. . . . Each child. Instantly loved. Permanently loved. To each he assigns a time. To each he appoints a place. No accidents. No coincidences. Just design.

The Author makes a promise to these unborn: *In my image, I will make you. You will be like me. You will laugh. You will create. You will never die. And you will write.*

They must. For each life is a book, not to be read, but rather a story to be written. The Author starts each life story, but each life will write his or her own ending.

What a dangerous liberty. How much safer it would have been to finish the story for each Adam. To script every option. It would have been simpler. It would have been safer. But it would not have been love. Love is only love if chosen.

So the Author decides to give each child a pen. "Write carefully," he whispers.

A Gentle Thunder

YOU **God's Brand-New Idea**

Acknowledgements

rateful acknowledgment is made to the following publishers for permission to reprint this copyrighted material. All copyrights are held by the author, Max Lucado.

And the Angels Were Silent (Nashville: W Publishing Group, 2003).

Come Thirsty (Nashville: W Publishing Group, 2004).

Cure for the Common Life (Nashville: W Publishing Group, 2005).

A Gentle Thunder (Nashville: W Publishing, 1995).

God Came Near (Nashville: W Publishing Group, 1987).

He Chose the Nails (Nashville: W Publishing Group, 2000).

In the Grip of Grace (Nashville: W Publishing Group, 1996).

It's Not About You (Nashville: Integrity Publishers, 2004)

Just Like Jesus (Nashville: W Publishing Group, 1998).

A Love Worth Giving (Nashville: W Publishing Group, 2002).

Next Door Savior (Nashville: W Publishing Group, 2003).

No Wonder They Call Him the Savior (Nashville: W Publishing Group, 2003).

Six Hours One Friday (Nashville: W Publishing Group, 1989).

Traveling Light (Nashville: W Publishing Group, 2000).

When God Whispers Your Name (Nashville: W Publishing Group, 1994).